# Lifted Up

Written by ASHLEY GOODEN

Scriptures taken from the Holy Bible, New International Version®, NIV®. Copyright © 1973, 1978, 1984, 2011 by Biblica, Inc.™ Used by permission of Zondervan. All rights reserved worldwide. www.zondervan.com The "NIV" and "New International Version" are trademarks registered in the United States Patent and Trademark Office by Biblica, Inc.

WestBow Press books may be ordered through booksellers or by contacting:

WestBow Press
A Division of Thomas Nelson & Zondervan
1663 Liberty Drive
Bloomington, IN 47403
www.westbowpress.com
1 (866) 928-1240

Because of the dynamic nature of the Internet, any web addresses or links contained in this book may have changed since publication and may no longer be valid. The views expressed in this work are solely those of the author and do not necessarily reflect the views of the publisher, and the publisher hereby disclaims any responsibility for them.

ISBN: 978-1-9736-3962-6 (sc)
ISBN: 978-1-9736-3963-3 (e)

Library of Congress Control Number: 2018911150

Print information available on the last page.

WestBow Press rev. date: 09/25/2018

# Dedication

To my wonderful husband, Kenan. Thank you for
loving and supporting me. This book is also written
for all my children. Mama loves you so much!

When the sun comes up, it is time to head to the ranch. LIFTED UP into the pickup to head down the dusty, dirt road.

Gates are opened and we are ready to start. Buckets get filled with grain and are LIFTED UP with little hands to be delivered to the calves.

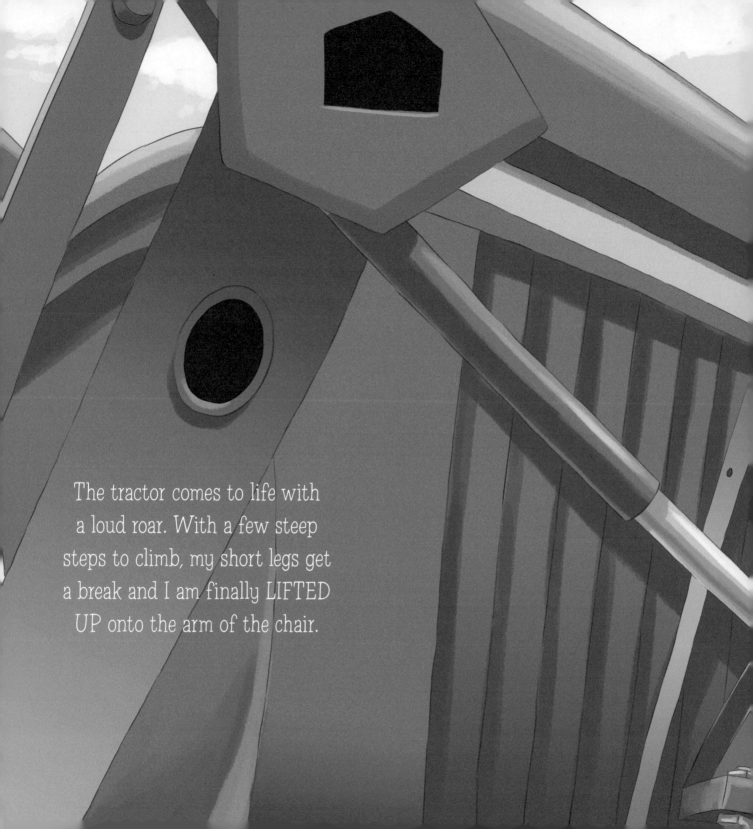

The tractor comes to life with
a loud roar. With a few steep
steps to climb, my short legs get
a break and I am finally LIFTED
UP onto the arm of the chair.

Bales are LIFTED UP and carried to
the feeders where they are dropped
and the cattle come running.

As Daddy waits with open arms,
I am LIFTED UP on his shoulders
for a walk through the fields.

I am LIFTED UP onto the large, round
bale while he cuts the string, surrounded
by the cattle waiting to eat.

Danger in sight! Out of nowhere I am
LIFTED UP out of harm's way!

After the work is done, we sit down and quench our thirst
as the jug of water is LIFTED UP to our mouths.

We sit and reflect on how good God is to us and how He has LIFTED us out of a life of sin.

Jesus was LIFTED UP on a cross and died for our sins because He loves you and me!

The story didn't end there. Daddy told me that Jesus rose from the dead and was LIFTED UP into the sky!

My Daddy won't always be here to LIFT me UP,
but there is one who always will...

God has and always will LIFT me UP. "The LORD upholds all those who fall and lifts up all who are bowed down." Psalm 145:14 NIV

## God, Please Lift Me Up

God, please lift me up when I am down,
When I do wrong and make you frown.
Lift me up when I cry,
To do good and really try.
Lift me up when I fear,
Helping me know that you are near.
Lifting me is what you do,
You have promised me, and I know it's true.
Your love for me is beyond compare,
By what Jesus did, I know you care!

— Ashley Gooden

Dear Readers,

We live in a life full of sin. We make wrong choices and sometimes disobey our parents. This makes God sad, but He never stops loving us. We can't earn our way to heaven or try to make up for the bad things we have done. There is only one way. God sent His only son, Jesus, to come to earth and die on a cross. Jesus never did anything wrong. Yet He still chose to pay the price for us and our wrong decisions. Jesus didn't stay in His grave, but is alive! After three days, He was lifted up into heaven! In heaven there will be no tears, no pain, and it will be more beautiful than we can imagine. If you believe this and ask Him to live in your heart, then you get to go to heaven and be with Him! What a wonderful gift!! I pray that you know how much God loves you and that when you are sad, mad, scared, feeling down, or needing His help...God will lift you up!!

"For God so loved the world that He gave His one and only Son, that whoever believes in Him shall not perish but have eternal life." John 3:16

Printed in the United States
By Bookmasters